joyfulsaintspress.com

WANT FREE COLORING PAGES?

Go to https://bit.ly/36hG5GL to sign up & download

Copyright © 2023 by Caitlyn L Ashleigh
ALL RIGHTS RESERVED

2024 Come Follow Me Old Testament Schedule

- ❏ Jan 1–7: Introductory Pages of the Book of Mormon
- ❏ Jan 8-14: 1 Nephi 1-5
- ❏ Jan 15-21: 1 Nephi 6-10
- ❏ Jan 22-28: 1 Nephi 11-15
- ❏ Jan 29-Feb 4: 1 Nephi 16-22
- ❏ Feb 5-11: 2 Nephi 1-2
- ❏ Feb 12-18: 2 Nephi 3-5
- ❏ Feb 19-25: 2 Nephi 6-10
- ❏ Feb 26 - Mar 3: 2 Nephi 11-19
- ❏ Mar 4-10: 2 Nephi 20-25
- ❏ Mar 11-17: 2 Nephi 26-30
- ❏ Mar 18-24: 2 Nephi 31-33
- ❏ Mar 25-31: Easter
- ❏ Apr 1-7: Jacob 1-4
- ❏ Apr 8-14: Jacob 5-7
- ❏ Apr 15-21: Enos-Words of Mormon
- ❏ Apr 22-28: Mosiah 1-3
- ❏ Apr 29 - May 5: Mosiah 4-6
- ❏ May 6-12: Mosiah 7-10
- ❏ May 13-19: Mosiah 11-17
- ❏ May 20-26: Mosiah 18-24
- ❏ May 27 – Jun 2 - Mosiah 25-28
- ❏ Jun 3-9: Mosiah 29 – Alma 4
- ❏ Jun 10-16: Alma 5-7
- ❏ Jun 17-23: Alma 8-12
- ❏ Jun 24-30: Alma 13-16
- ❏ Jul 1 - Jul 7: Alma 17-22
- ❏ Jul 8-14: Alma 23-29
- ❏ Jul 15-21: Alma 30-31
- ❏ Jul 22-28: Alma 32-35
- ❏ Jul 29-Aug 4: Alma 36-38
- ❏ Aug 5-11: Alma 39-42
- ❏ Aug 12-18: Alma 43-52
- ❏ Aug 19-25: Alma 53-63
- ❏ Aug 26-Sep 1: Helaman 1-6
- ❏ Sep 2-8: Helaman 7-12
- ❏ Sep 9-15: Helaman 13-16
- ❏ Sep 16-22: 3 Nephi 1-7
- ❏ Sep 23-29: 3 Nephi 8-11
- ❏ Sep 30-Oct 6: 3 Nephi 12-16
- ❏ Oct 7-13: 3 Nephi 17-19
- ❏ Oct 14-20: 3 Nephi 20-26
- ❏ Oct 21-27: 3 Nephi 27 – 4 Nephi
- ❏ Oct 28-Nov 3: Mormon 1-6
- ❏ Nov 4-10: Mormon 7-9
- ❏ Nov 11-17: Ether 1-5
- ❏ Nov 18-24: Ether 6-11
- ❏ Nov 25 – Dec 1: Ether 12-15
- ❏ Dec 2-8: Moroni 1-6
- ❏ Dec 9-15: Moroni 7-9
- ❏ Dec 16-22: Moroni 10
- ❏ Dec 23-29: Christmas

MY TESTIMONY

MY FAMILY CIRCLE

I AM SURROUNDED BY LOVE AND MY FAMILY. I AM NOT ALONE IN MY JOURNEY TO BECOME MORE LIKE JESUS CHRIST.

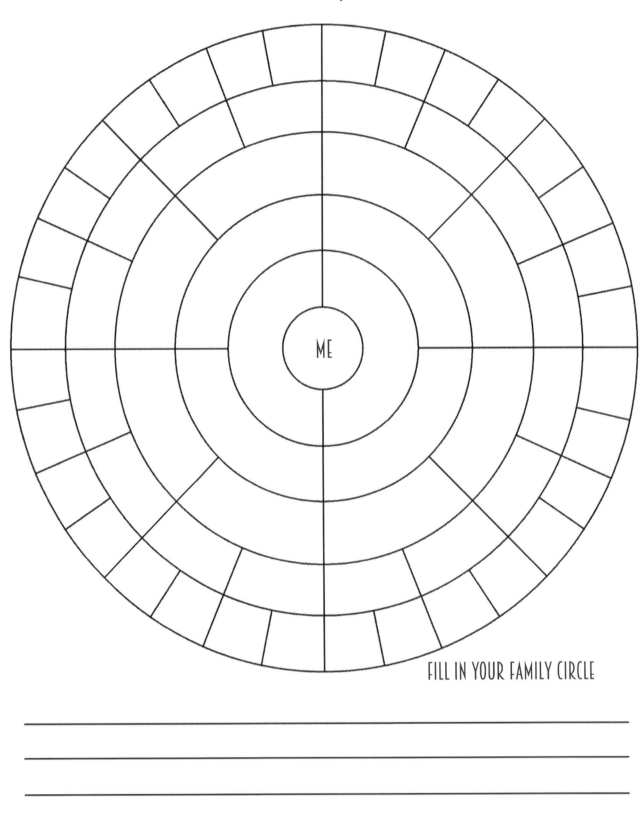

FILL IN YOUR FAMILY CIRCLE

MY GOALS THIS YEAR

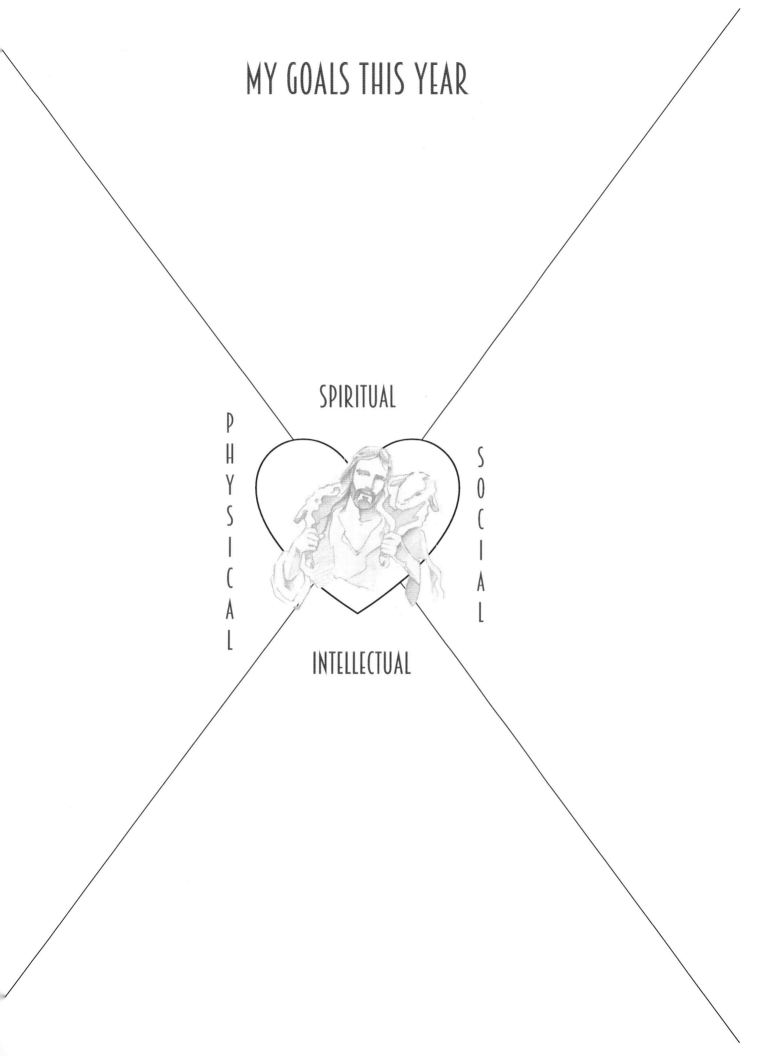

Color the books of the Book of Mormon as you read them

Jan 1-7

Monday — Title Page How is the Book of Mormon different from other scriptures?

Tuesday — Introduction How does the history of the Book of Mormon demonstrate Heavenly Father's love?

Wednesday — Testimony of the 3 & 8 Witnesses How do the witnesses' testimonies inspire me to share my testimony?

Thursday — Testimony of the Prophet Joseph Smith What about Joseph Smith's experience/testimony speaks of truth and Heavenly Father's love?

Introductory Pages of the Book of Mormon

Friday

Brief Explanation of the Book of Mormon Did I learn anything new about the Book of Mormon?

Saturday

What is my plan for scripture study this year and my main goal?

Sunday Reflection

Spiritual Promptings

Goal for Next Week

Jan 8-14

Monday — 1 Nephi 1 What hard thing(s) has the Lord asked me to do? Did I do them, even if I might be mocked?

Tuesday — 1 Nephi 2 When has prayer softened my heart and drawn me closer to Heavenly Father?

Wednesday — 1 Nephi 3 Why are the words of the prophets, past and present, precious to me?

Thursday — 1 Nephi 4:1-18 When have I been "led by the spirit?"

1 Nephi 1-5

Friday — 1 Nephi 4:19-38 How did the Lord "prepare a way" for me, like Nephi, to accomplish something hard?

Saturday — 1 Nephi 5 When have I complained against the Lord? What did I learn?

Sunday Reflection

Spiritual Promptings

Goal for Next Week

Jan 15-21

Monday — 1 Nephi 6 How can I think more often of what is "pleasing unto God" instead of the world?

Tuesday — 1 Nephi 7 Have I ever forgotten the "great thing the Lord hath done" for me?

Wednesday — 1 Nephi 8:1-18 How would partaking of the fruit of the tree bring me joy?

Thursday — 1 Nephi 8:19-38 What helps me cling to the iron rod? How can I help others do the same?

1 Nephi 6-10

Friday — 1 Nephi 9 Have I followed a personal revelation that led to a "wise purpose"?

Saturday — 1 Nephi 10 What am I desirous to see, hear, or know for myself? What can I pray for today to understand?

Sunday Reflection

Spiritual Promptings

Goal for Next Week

Jan 22-28

Monday — 1 Nephi 11 How can my Savior's example help me feel the love of God and forget about my own pride?

Tuesday — 1 Nephi 12 What have I learned about the Savior from Nephi's vision?

Wednesday — 1 Nephi 13:1-19 How can I humble myself so that "the power of the Lord" is with me?

Thursday — 1 Nephi 13:20-42 How does Jesus Christ help me avoid the captivity of false ideas?

1 Nephi 11-15

Friday — 1 Nephi 14 What "great and marvelous" things has the Lord done for me?

Saturday — 1 Nephi 15 How can Nephi's entreaty to seek with a humble heart, faith, diligence, and believing I will receive help?

Sunday Reflection

Spiritual Promptings

Goal for Next Week

Jan 29 - Feb 4

Monday — 1 Nephi 16 When has the Lord guided and led me through challenges?

Tuesday — 1 Nephi 17 What recent trial can I look at from the perspective of faith and gratitude?

Wednesday — 1 Nephi 18 How can I be more like Nephi who praised the Lord after being set free?

Thursday — 1 Nephi 19 How have Nephi's writings helped me to "remember the Lord" my Redeemer?

1 Nephi 16-22

Friday — 1 Nephi 20-21 How does the light of Christ "feed" me and make my heart sing with joy?

Saturday — 1 Nephi 22 How can the phrase "the righteous need not fear" comfort me in times of trouble?

Sunday Reflection

Spiritual Promptings

Goal for Next Week

Feb 5-11

Monday — 2 Nephi 1:1-9 What blessings has the Lord promised me if I keep His commandments?

Tuesday — 2 Nephi 1:10-20 What can help me awaken from a spiritual "deep sleep" and throw off spiritual "chains"?

Wednesday — 2 Nephi 1:21-32 What can I do today/this week to be more of "one mind and in one heart" with my fellow man?

Thursday — 2 Nephi 2:1-10 Why is it important for me to know good from evil?

2 Nephi 1-2

Friday — 2 Nephi 2:11-20 Why is agency so important to Heavenly Father?

Saturday — 2 Nephi 2:21-30 What joy have I experienced due to opposition?

Sunday Reflection

Spiritual Promptings

Goal for Next Week

Feb 12-18

Monday — 2 Nephi 3:1-11 What work or service can I do today to be "great" in the eyes of the Lord?

Tuesday — 2 Nephi 3:12-25 How is my life different because the Lord restored His church through Joseph Smith?

Wednesday — 2 Nephi 4:1-16 Does my "soul delighteth in the things of the Lord"? What does my "heart pondereth" today?

Thursday — 2 Nephi 4:17-35 Even Nephi was tempted to sin, what can I learn from his struggles?

2 Nephi 3-5

Friday — 2 Nephi 5:1-17 When has observing the commandments of Heavenly Father allow me to prosper?

Saturday — 2 Nephi 5:18-34 What can I change right now that would help me better live in the manner of happiness?

Sunday Reflection

Spiritual Promptings

Goal for Next Week

Feb 19-25

Monday — 2 Nephi 6 Are my daily prayers the "prayers of the faithful" or have my prayers become routine?

Tuesday — 2 Nephi 7 What can I do or change today to "walk in the light?"

Wednesday — 2 Nephi 8 What does the Savior offer me if I seek Him?

Thursday — 2 Nephi 9:1-26 Why do I personally need Christ's Atonement?

2 Nephi 6-10

Friday — 2 Nephi 9:27-54 When has Satan tried to lead me away from God's plan?

Saturday — 2 Nephi 10 What ideas or concept of God's plan "cheer up" my heart?

Sunday Reflection

Spiritual Promptings

Goal for Next Week

Feb 26 - Mar 3

Monday

2 Nephi 11-12 What will help me avoid dwindling in unbelief and remembering Christ?

Tuesday

2 Nephi 13-14 Where do I see pride hurting people? How can I be more humble?

Wednesday

2 Nephi 15 What vices hold me captive? What is one thing I can do to free myself?

Thursday

2 Nephi 16-17 Christ miraculous birth was a sign unto men so they would believe. What signs have increased my faith?

2 Nephi 11-19

Friday — 2 Nephi 18 When has my testimony helped me avoid stumbling and losing faith?

Saturday — 2 Nephi 19 When has thinking of Christ's birth brought my soul great joy?

Sunday Reflection

Spiritual Promptings

Goal for Next Week

Mar 4 - 10

Monday — 2 Nephi 20 How can I be a "light of Israel" and share the light of Christ?

Tuesday — 2 Nephi 21 What do I think the gathering of Israel looks like? How can I help?

Wednesday — 2 Nephi 22 Spend a few minute thinking about meeting Christ. What would living with Him feel like?

Thursday — 2 Nephi 23 How can I be more worthy of God's mercy?

2 Nephi 20-25

Friday — 2 Nephi 24 When has following the commandments given me rest from sorrow or fear?

Saturday — 2 Nephi 25 How do Nephi's words help me more clearly understand Isaiah?

Sunday Reflection

Spiritual Promptings

Goal for Next Week

Mar 11 - 17

Monday — 2 Nephi 26:1-13 What choice can I make today that is a choice for light rather than darkness?

Tuesday — 2 Nephi 26:14-35 What examples have I seen that prove that the Lord "loveth the world"?

Wednesday — 2 Nephi 27 Do I feel that the Book of Mormon is a marvelous work? Why?

Thursday — 2 Nephi 28 When has Satan tried to convince me that "a little sin" is okay?

2 Nephi 26-30

Friday — 2 Nephi 29 What marvelous works and wonders have I witnessed yet the world doesn't see them?

Saturday — 2 Nephi 30 What little change can I make today so that Satan shall have no power over my heart?

Sunday Reflection

Spiritual Promptings

Goal for Next Week

Mar 18-24

Monday — 2 Nephi 31:1-12 Why was Christ baptized? Why was I baptized?

Tuesday — 2 Nephi 31:13-21 How do I know I am enduring to the end? What helps me when I falter?

Wednesday — 2 Nephi 32:1-4 What words of Christ should I ponder in my heart today?

Thursday — 2 Nephi 32:5-9 Today can I "harken unto the Spirit" so I know what to pray for?

2 Nephi 31-33

Friday — 2 Nephi 33:1-5 What has the power to harden my heart? How can I guard against that?

Saturday — 2 Nephi 33:6-15 How can I cultivate a Christ-like spirit of charity in my life?

Sunday Reflection

Spiritual Promptings

Goal for Next Week

Mar 25 - 31

Monday
Book of Mormon Title page; Jacob 4:3-4 How do these testimonies of a resurrected Christ strengthen my own testimony?

Tuesday
2 Nephi 9:6-15; 22; Alma 11:42-45 What truths about the resurrection do I learn from these scriptures?

Wednesday
Alma 40:21-25; 3 Nephi 26:4-5 How does understanding the resurrection influence my life?

Thursday
Hymn 136 I Know My Redeemer Lives; Gospel Library – Easter Videos What about this hymn and videos is meaningful to me?

Easter

Friday

Mosiah 3:7; 15:5-9; Alma 7:11-13 What does Christ suffering mean to me?

Saturday

Mosiah 5:1-2; 27:8-28; Alma 15:3-12; 24:7-19 What do each of these experience have in common? Differences?

Sunday Reflection

Spiritual Promptings

Goal for Next Week

My Testimony of this Conference

Notes

Apr 1-7

Monday — Jacob 2:1-16 When have I "labored diligently" for the Lord?

Tuesday — Jacob 2:17-35 Do I seek to help others with my talents and/or riches?

Wednesday — Jacob 3 How can I be more pure of heart?

Thursday — Jacob 4:1-8 How can my weaknesses teach me more about the Lord's love?

Jacob 1-4

Friday — Jacob 4:9-18 When have I felt the "spirit of truth" speak to me?

Saturday — What in these verses (Jacob 1-4) inspired me the most this week?

Sunday Reflection

Spiritual Promptings

Goal for Next Week

Apr 8-14

Monday — Jacob 5:1-28 What symbols in this story resonate with me?

Tuesday — Jacob 5:29-51 What do you learn about Christ from these verses?

Wednesday — Jacob 5:52-77 What have I learned about Christ by helping Him in His vineyard (His work)?

Thursday — Jacob 6 What evil fruits have I cast into the fire? Or what can I cast into the fire to help me feel Christ's love?

Jacob 5-7

Friday — Jacob 7:1-12 When have I been led away from the right by flattery? What have I learned?

Saturday — Jacob 7:13-27 Do I need a sign to truly know God? What small inconsequential signs have I witnessed?

Sunday Reflection

Spiritual Promptings

Goal for Next Week

Apr 15-21

Monday — Enos 1:1-13 Has my soul ever hungered as I knelt to pray?

Tuesday — Enos 1:14-27 Has my faith ever been as strong as Enos? If not, how can I strengthen it?

Wednesday — Jarom How does the world's definition of prosperity differ from God's?

Thursday — Omni 1:1-11 When have I seen that not following the commandments has led to a lack of prosperity?

Enos-Words of Mormon

Friday — Omni 1:12-30 What would offering my whole soul unto Christ be like?

Saturday — The Words of Mormon What have I learned from Mormon's compilation of 1 Nephi – Omni?

Sunday Reflection

Spiritual Promptings

Goal for Next Week

Apr 22-28

Monday — Mosiah 1:1-8 What profound truth has scripture study and searching the Book of Mormon diligently taught me?

Tuesday — Mosiah 1:9-18 The Liahona stopped leading people if they were unfaithful. What indicators in my life pointed out when I needed more faith?

Wednesday — Mosiah 2:1-26 What truth did King Benjamin teach that inspires me to serve others?

Thursday — Mosiah 2:27-41 What does happiness that comes from obedience to God feel like?

Mosiah 1-3

Friday — Mosiah 3:1-12 How does knowing that Christ suffered earthly temptations and pain help me come closer to Christ?

Saturday — Mosiah 3:13-27 How can I be more child-like in my love for Christ?

Sunday Reflection

Spiritual Promptings

Goal for Next Week

April 29 – May 5

Monday

Mosiah 4:1-10 What condition does God require to grant remission of my sins?

Tuesday

Mosiah 4:11-20 Have I experienced "exceedingly great joy" from repentance?

Wednesday

Mosiah 4:21-30 What checks and balances do I have in place to watch my thoughts, words, and deeds?

Thursday

Mosiah 5:1-5 What helps remind me to "do good continually"?

Mosiah 4-6

Friday — Mosiah 5:6-15 What does it mean to me to "retain the name written always in your heart"?

Saturday — Mosiah 6 What do I feel is wise about Mosiah desiring to "not become burdensome" to his people?

Sunday Reflection

Spiritual Promptings

Goal for Next Week

May 6-12

Monday — Mosiah 7:1-15 When have I sought out someone who has been lost?

Tuesday — Mosiah 7:16-33 When in my sadness or despair have I turned to the Lord with full purpose of heart? What happened?

Wednesday — Mosiah 8 Why were seers important in the Book of Mormon times and in our time?

Thursday — Mosiah 9:1-9 When have I been slow to remember the Lord?

Mosiah 7-10

Friday — Mosiah 9:10-19 What has motivated me in the past to remember the Lord and cry mightily unto Him?

Saturday — Mosiah 10 The Lamanites past choices effected their future generations. What does that suggest about my choices?

Sunday Reflection

Spiritual Promptings

Goal for Next Week

May 13-19

Monday — Mosiah 11 How does Abinadi's courage to speak out against King Noah inspire me?

Tuesday — Mosiah 12 When is it important to "apply my heart to understanding"? When has the gospel confused me?

Wednesday — Mosiah 13 Are the commandments written on my heart? Are there commandments that I still need to work on?

Thursday — Mosiah 14 What phases or images in these verses deepen my love for Christ?

Mosiah 11-17

Friday — Mosiah 15 What insights about Christ do I gain from Abinadi's testimony?

Saturday — Mosiah 16-17 What would it feel like to be "endlessly lost"? Does that give me a better appreciation for Christ's redemption?

Sunday Reflection

Spiritual Promptings

Goal for Next Week

May 20-26

Monday — Mosiah 18 What promises did I make during my baptism? What promises did God make to me?

Tuesday — Mosiah 19 Who in this story of Gideon, King Noah, Limhi, and the Nephites do I identify with the most?

Wednesday — Mosiah 20 What would I fight for with the fierceness of a dragon?

Thursday — Mosiah 21 When I lack humility is God slow to hear my cries?

Mosiah 18-24

Friday — Mosiah 22-23 Why did Alma not want to be king? What can I learn from that?

Saturday — Mosiah 24 When has faith and prayer made my burdens light?

Sunday Reflection

Spiritual Promptings

Goal for Next Week

May 27 - Jun 2

Monday — Mosiah 25 Did my baptism make me feel like I belong to the Church of God? What other things make me feel like I belong?

Tuesday — Mosiah 26:1-17 When recently have I poured out my soul to God?

Wednesday — Mosiah 26:18-39 How does forgiving others give me insights into God's forgiveness of my trespasses?

Thursday — Mosiah 27:1-19 Who might pray for me as Alma's parents did? Who can I pray for?

Mosiah 25-28

Friday

Mosiah 27:20-39 Alma's conversion was dramatic, but what big or small things played a part in my conversion?

Saturday

Mosiah 28 When I am hesitant to share the gospel, what can give me courage like the sons of Mosiah?

Sunday Reflection

Spiritual Promptings

Goal for Next Week

Jun 3-9

Monday — Mosiah 29:1-24 Do I truly believe it is better to be judged of God than man?

Tuesday — Mosiah 29:25-47 The people had "voices" in who would be judges. Why is it important to have a voice in my leaders?

Wednesday — Alma 1 What have I learned from living or deceased prophets that refute today's false teachings?

Thursday — Alma 2 What "mighty prayers" might I reap according to my works?

Mosiah 29 – Alma 4

Friday — Alma 3 What rewards might I reap according to my works?

Saturday — Alma 4 When have I worried about loved ones struggles? How did or can I help?

Sunday Reflection

Spiritual Promptings

Goal for Next Week

June 10-16

Monday — Alma 5:1-20 What things or actions keep me in bondage? What could I change to deliver my soul?

Tuesday — Alma 5:21-42 Have I felt a change of heart and felt Christ's song of redeeming love?

Wednesday — Alma 5:43-62 What truths of the gospel and things can I do to seek for truth and grow my testimony?

Thursday — Alma 6 Who can I pray and fast for to know the gospel?

Alma 5-7

Friday

Alma 7:1-16 How can understanding Christ and His sacrifices for me help comfort me when I feel as if no one understands?

Saturday

Alma 7:17-27 Alma offers a list of things to come unto Christ; humble, gentle, patient, etc. What can I work on?

Sunday Reflection

Spiritual Promptings

Goal for Next Week

Jun 17-23

Monday — Alma 8 Have I shared the gospel with friends and felt rejected? Does Alma's experience help comfort me?

Tuesday — Alma 9 What great blessing and corresponding responsibilities has God given me?

Wednesday — Alma 10 What are the blessings of a humble and softened heart? When have I experienced this?

Thursday — Alma 11:1-20 Have I ever stirred up contention for my own purposes? Pride? Revenge? Spite?

Alma 8-12

Friday

Alma 11:21-46 What effect does Amulek testimony of Christ and the Plan of Salvation have on me?

Saturday

Alma 12 How can I avoid a hardened heart and instead turn it toward God?

Sunday Reflection

Spiritual Promptings

Goal for Next Week

Jun 24-30

Monday — Alma 13:1-13 What role or blessing has the Priesthood played in my life?

Tuesday — Alma 13:14-31 Do I procrastinate the day of my repentance? What one thing can I do or change today to improve?

Wednesday — Alma 14:1-17 Blessings for faith are not always awarded in this life. What can motivate me to keep faith even without immediate results?

Thursday — Alma 14:18-29 We may never be freed from an actual prison, but what spiritual prisons has faith freed me from?

Alma 13-16

Friday — Alma 15 What about ZeeZrom's change of heart inspired or lifts me up?

Saturday — Alma 16 What would it be like to have the Lord pour out His Spirit on me? Am I prepared for something like that?

Sunday Reflection

Spiritual Promptings

Goal for Next Week

Jul 1-7

Monday — Alma 17 How can I keep my testimony strong based on the testimonies of Alma and the sons of Mosiah?

Tuesday — Alma 18 What events or experiences has made a great impact on my conversion to the gospel?

Wednesday — Alma 19 What did I learn about Christ and His character from these verses?

Thursday — Alma 20 What am I willing to sacrifice to know God more deeply?

Alma 17-22

Friday — Alma 21 If I examine the "intent of my heart" today what do I find?

Saturday — Alma 22 How can Aaron's joy and excitement sharing the gospel inspire me?

Sunday Reflection

Spiritual Promptings

Goal for Next Week

Jul 8-14

Monday — Alma 23 What is similar between my conversion "unto the Lord" and the Anti-Nephi-Lehies?

Tuesday — Alma 24 What "weapons," harsh thoughts, sins, etc. have I put away to follow Christ?

Wednesday — Alma 25 In what ways do I "walk in the ways of the Lord"?

Thursday — Alma 26 What would the "marvelous light of God" feel like? How did Ammon express his joy?

Alma 23-29

Friday — Alma 27 Do I welcome and protect those that were once enemies? Do I forgive other easily?

Saturday — Alma 28-29 There is sorrow and joy in this life. Does understanding "the light of Christ" help put that in perspective?

Sunday Reflection

Spiritual Promptings

Goal for Next Week

Jul 15-21

Monday — Alma 30:1-18 What false doctrine do I see in these verses?

Tuesday — Alma 30:19-29 What false thing(s) did Korihor say that might be tempting to believe?

Wednesday — Alma 30:30-45 Even with the gospel laid out before me, what teaching do I still need to increase my faith??

Thursday — Alma 30:46-60 Korihor received his sign. What things might I be stubborn about?

Alma 30-31

Friday

Alma 31:1-22 When have I witnessed the word of God being more powerful than "anything else"?

Saturday

Alma 31:23-38 Have my prayers become repetitious, prideful, or vain?

Sunday Reflection

Spiritual Promptings

Goal for Next Week

Jul 22-28

Monday — Alma 32:1-17 When has being "lowly in heart" been a blessing to me?

Tuesday — Alma 32:18-43 What did I learn about faith and how to exercise it?

Wednesday — Alma 33 What is prayer and worship? How can I incorporate it more fully into my life?

Thursday — Alma 34:1-17 Why is it important for me to understand that the Atonement is infinite and eternal?

Alma 32-35

Friday — Alma 34:18-41 Is it ever too late to repent? How wonderful would an immediate "relief from the burdens" of the world be?

Saturday — Alma 35 What can I do this week "to receive the poor" or "nourish" the souls around me?

Sunday Reflection

Spiritual Promptings

Goal for Next Week

Jul 29 - Aug 4

Monday — Alma 36:1-15 When has God supported me in my trials and lifted me up?

Tuesday — Alma 36:16-30 What does it mean to be born of God? How does this knowledge offer me perspective?

Wednesday — Alma 37:1-14 When have I witnessed the principle "by small and simple things are great things brought to pass"?

Thursday — Alma 37:15-31 In what ways am I successful in fulfilling the commandments? What are my wins?

Alma 36-38

Friday — Alma 37:32-47 When have I become slothful because of the easiness of the way? What can keep me on track?

Saturday — Alma 38 What personal counsel do I gain from Alma's advice to Shiblon?

Sunday Reflection

Spiritual Promptings

Goal for Next Week

Aug 5-11

Monday — Alma 39 Why is it important to keep my thoughts and actions chaste?

Tuesday — Alma 40 How can Alma's example of seeking for answers help me this day or week?

Wednesday — Alma 41 What thoughts do I have on the phrase "wickedness never was happiness"?

Thursday — Alma 42:1-14 How does the idea that life is a probationary time offer me perspective?

Alma 39-42

Friday — Alma 42:15-31 Why is opposition to the Plan of Happiness necessary?

Saturday — Read Alma 42 again. How does Christ's Atonement make justice and mercy possible?

Sunday Reflection

Spiritual Promptings

Goal for Next Week

Aug 12-18

Monday

Alma 43 How does Alma's account of his people's wars prepare me for the battles in my everyday life?

Tuesday

Alma 44-45 Does the Nephite's desire to defend their faith and freedom inspire me to share the gospel?

Wednesday

Alma 46-47 What do I picture when I imagine the Title of Liberty? What do I feel when I imagine it?

Thursday

Alma 48-49 What can I do to strengthen myself and "prepare my mind" to defend against worldliness?

Alma 43-52

Friday — Alma 50-51 When has my own stubbornness gotten in the way of doing/choosing the right?

Saturday — Alma 52 How has planning, preparation, and prayer helped me succeed?

Sunday Reflection

Spiritual Promptings

Goal for Next Week

Aug 19-25

Monday — Alma 53-54 What would valiance, courage, strength, soberness, and truthful actions look like in today's world?

Tuesday — Alma 55; 56:1-26 Moroni armed the prisoners instead of slaying the drunken Lamanites, what does this teach me about mercy?

Wednesday — Alma 56:27-57; 57 When has faith and a firmness of mind helped me?

Thursday — Alma 58-59 Support can often seem far away. What can help me remember to pour out my soul in prayer?

Alma 53-63

Friday — Alma 60-61 How should I care for people in need?

Saturday — Alma 62-63 When have challenges hardened my heart? Or softened my heart?

Sunday Reflection

Spiritual Promptings

Goal for Next Week

Aug 26 – Sep 1

Monday — Helaman 1 Can I see how the people's contentions weakened the Nephites? How can contention weaken me?

Tuesday — Helaman 2 The desire for power can lead to ruin. What can help align my desires with God's?

Wednesday — Helaman 3 How can I recognize in myself when the joy of blessings might slip toward pride?

Thursday — Helaman 4 Where can I see the pride cycle throughout these verses?

Helaman 1-6

Friday — Helaman 5 What does building a firm foundation look like to me?

Saturday — Helaman 6 What can I do this week that would help lift up the poor or meek instead of trampling them?

Sunday Reflection

Spiritual Promptings

Goal for Next Week

Sep 2-8

Monday
Helaman 7 Why is listening to the voice of the prophets wise?

Tuesday
Helaman 8 Looking toward Moses's serpent or toward Christ seems simple, but how is following Christ a constant desire to recommit?

Wednesday
Helaman 9 Would it be easy for me to dismiss a miracle as something explained by science?

Thursday
Helaman 10 How did Nephi gain the Lord's trust and what does that teach me?

Helaman 7-12

Friday — Helaman 11 How have my recent trials effected my faith?

Saturday — Helaman 12 What can help me remember the Lord? What distractions can I avoid?

Sunday Reflection

Spiritual Promptings

Goal for Next Week

Sep 9-15

Monday — Helaman 13:1-17 When I pray, what has come "into my heart"?

Tuesday — Helaman 13:18-39 Do I or have I sought happiness "in doing inequity"?

Wednesday — Helaman 14:1-13 Why are the signs of the Savior's birth an effective way to announce His birth?

Thursday — Helaman 14:14-31 If I have been given the gift of knowledge of good and evil, how am I using that freedom?

Helaman 13-16

Friday — Helaman 15 How can the Lord's chastisement be a sign of His love?

Saturday — Helaman 16 What do I learn from people who accepted Samuel's teachings? Rejected Him?

Sunday Reflection

Spiritual Promptings

Goal for Next Week

Sep 16-22

Monday — 3 Nephi 1 How can the words "lift up your head and be of good cheer" inspire me?

Tuesday — 3 Nephi 2-3 When my beliefs are threatened what or who can help strengthened me?

Wednesday — 3 Nephi 4 When have I last truly praised the Lord with a full heart for His blessings?

Thursday — 3 Nephi 5 What does it mean to me to be a disciple of Christ?

3 Nephi 1-7

Friday — 3 Nephi 6 When has the trapping of the world or pride gotten in the way of my relationship with Christ?

Saturday — 3 Nephi 7 Have I ever been angry when I saw a miracle or when called to change my ways?

Sunday Reflection

Spiritual Promptings

Goal for Next Week

Sep 23-29

Monday — 3 Nephi 8 What brings light into my life?

Tuesday — 3 Nephi 9 Why does Christ want me to come to Him with a broken heart and contrite spirit?

Wednesday — 3 Nephi 10 How can I "repeat and return unto" Christ "with a full purpose of heart"?

Thursday — 3 Nephi 11:1-8 How can I "open my ears" to better hear the voice of God?

3 Nephi 8-11

Friday

3 Nephi 11:9-28 Why would Christ introduce himself as the light of the world?

Saturday

3 Nephi 11:29-41 What contention do I need to let go of?

Sunday Reflection

Spiritual Promptings

Goal for Next Week

Sep 30 – Oct 6

Monday: 3 Nephi 12:1-20 "Come unto me and be ye saved". What can I do today to follow the path?

Tuesday: 3 Nephi 12:21-48 How can I better love others even if they are wrong or hate me?

Wednesday: 3 Nephi 13 Have my prayers become routine? Do I truly seek to communicate with Heavenly Father?

Thursday: 3 Nephi 14 Which of Christ's admonishments do I need to work on?

3 Nephi 12-16

Friday — 3 Nephi 15 How can I be a light and testify of Christ?

Saturday — 3 Nephi 16 What does Christ's concern for His "other sheep" tell me about His nature?

Sunday Reflection

Spiritual Promptings

Goal for Next Week

My Testimony of this Conference

Notes

Oct 7-13

Monday — 3 Nephi 17:1-12 How does Christ's compassion to "tarry a little longer with them" make me feel?

Tuesday — 3 Nephi 17:13-25 Why do I think that Christ stated "now behold my joy is full"?

Wednesday — 3 Nephi 18:1-16 How can reading about Christ instituting the sacrament inspire me when I take the sacrament?

Thursday — 3 Nephi 18:17-39 How did Christ minister unto His people? What can I learn from His example?

3 Nephi 17-19

Friday

3 Nephi 19:1-18 Why was the gift of the Holy Ghost so desirable to the people?

Saturday

3 Nephi 19:19-36 What did I learn about faith and prayer from these verses?

Sunday Reflection

Spiritual Promptings

Goal for Next Week

Oct 14-20

Monday — 3 Nephi 20 When have I seen the power of the Lord work amongst His people?

Tuesday — 3 Nephi 21 Have I seen the truth of the prophesies of the spreading of the gospel in my lifetime? How?

Wednesday — 3 Nephi 22 How has tribulation and trials forged me into something better? How can I help in Christ's mission?

Thursday — 3 Nephi 23 If the Lord looked at my records what might He ask me?

3 Nephi 20-26

Friday — 3 Nephi 24-25 How can paying tithing open the windows of heaven? What blessings have I witnessed?

Saturday — 3 Nephi 26 How would I feel today if I was to "stand before God"?

Sunday Reflection

Spiritual Promptings

Goal for Next Week

Oct 21-27

Monday — 3 Nephi 27 Why is it important Christ's name is part of the church's name?

Tuesday — 3 Nephi 28:1-22 What do I desire of Christ? How does or can living the gospel change my desires?

Wednesday — 3 Nephi 28:23-40 What "great and marvelous works" have I witnesses? How did they testify of Christ?

Thursday — 3 Nephi 29-30 What things have I seen that show that God has begun gathering His people?

3 Nephi 27 – 4 Nephi

Friday

4 Nephi 1:1-23 What choices can I make that will help me live a blessed life like the Nephites?

Saturday

4 Nephi 1:24-49 How can contention destroy good works? How can I be a peacemaker?

Sunday Reflection

Spiritual Promptings

Goal for Next Week

Oct 28 - Nov 3

Monday

Mormon 1 How would I feel if the Holy Ghost was taken from me?

Tuesday

Mormon 2 What is the difference between godly sorrow and worldly sorrow?

Wednesday

Mormon 3 The Nephites didn't acknowledge God's blessings. How am I acknowledging His blessing in my life?

Thursday

Mormon 4 How can I avoid delighting in wickedness? Even small temptations?

Mormon 1-6

Friday — Mormon 5 When I see the world turning to wickedness how can prayer help? Has it in the past?

Saturday — Mormon 6 If Christ stands with open arms, am I able to humble myself to reach out to Him?

Sunday Reflection

Spiritual Promptings

Goal for Next Week

Nov 4-10

Monday — Mormon 7 What does the phrase "hold upon the gospel of Christ" mean to me?

Tuesday — Mormon 8:1-22 Like Moroni, how can I remain faithful even when those around me do not?

Wednesday — Mormon 8:23-41 Which of Moroni's warnings for my day speak to me?

Thursday — Mormon 9:1-14 Is it comforting or upsetting that people will be who they were in life after the resurrection?

Mormon 7-9

Friday — Mormon 9:15-37 What do I learn about past and present miracles?

Saturday — Mormon and Moroni knew what it was like to be alone in a wicked world. How can Christ help me stay steadfast too?

Sunday Reflection

Spiritual Promptings

Goal for Next Week

Nov 11-17

Monday — Ether 1:1-32 What did I learn about the 24 plates and what Moroni abridged?

Tuesday — Ether 1:33-43 What did I learn about the land of promise? Why is it choice?

Wednesday — Ether 2 What did I learn from the Lord's response to the brother of Jared's prayer?

Thursday — Ether 3 How can the brother of Jared's great faith inspire my faith?

Ether 1-5

Friday — Ether 4 What might prevent me from receiving revelation? How can I improve?

Saturday — Ether 5 Why did the Lord prepare so many witnesses of the Book of Mormon?

Sunday Reflection

Spiritual Promptings

Goal for Next Week

Nov 18-24

Monday

Ether 6 How is my life journey like the brother of Jared's journey with the Lord leading us all to the promised land?

Tuesday

Ether 7 What can I learn about Christ-like leadership from Shule?

Wednesday

Ether 8 What is so destructive about secret combinations?

Thursday

Ether 9 What were the emotions of the rulers and how did that effect the people?

Ether 6-11

Friday — Ether 10 What did the righteous kings remember?

Saturday — Ether 11 The Jaredite's received mercy when they repented. Do I feel the Lord's mercy when I repent?

Sunday Reflection

Spiritual Promptings

Goal for Next Week

Nov 25 – Dec 1

Monday

Ether 12:1-21 What reasons did Ether have "hope for a better world"? Why would I hope?

Tuesday

Ether 12:22-41 How, like Moroni, can my weaknesses be turned into a strength for the Lord?

Wednesday

Ether 13 What did Ether counsel Coriantumr to do to protect himself? How does that advice apply to me?

Thursday

Ether 14 How does the state of the Jaredites during these verses make me feel? How can I defend against this in my life?

Ether 12-15

Friday — Ether 15:1-14 How did loss soften Coriantumr's heart? Has loss softened mine?

Saturday — Ether 15:15-34 How did anger, bitterness, and pride block the Spirit from the Jaredites?

Sunday Reflection

Spiritual Promptings

Goal for Next Week

Dec 2-8

Monday — Moroni 1 What are ways one might "deny Christ"? What can help me remain faithful?

Tuesday — Moroni 2 How has the power of the Holy Ghost cleansed or helped me?

Wednesday — Moroni 3 What could help someone prepare to be ordained to the priesthood? How could those activities help me?

Thursday — Moroni 4 What can I do to make the sacrament the spiritual highlight of my week?

Moroni 1-6

Friday — Moroni 5 What do I think about during the sacrament?

Saturday — Moroni 6 What might I need to work on to meet the qualifications of baptism?

Sunday Reflection

Spiritual Promptings

Goal for Next Week

Dec 9-15

Monday — Moroni 7:1-19 How do I know if my impressions come from my own thoughts or God?

Tuesday — Moroni 7:20-48 How is it possible through faith, hope, and charity to "lay hold" to good things?

Wednesday — Moroni 8:1-15 How can I be more like little children who are "whole" and "alive in Christ"?

Thursday — Moroni 8:16-30 What experiences have I had with the Holy Ghost being a "comforter filled with hope and perfect love"?

Moroni 7-9

Friday — Moroni 9:1-14 The Nephites experienced much hunger. What are some of the consequences of anger?

Saturday — Moroni 9:15-26 When times are troubled and wickedness surrounds me, how can "Christ lift thee up"?

Sunday Reflection

Spiritual Promptings

Goal for Next Week

Dec 16-22

Monday — Moroni 10:1-7 Have I accepted Moroni's invitation to ask God if the Book of Mormon true?

Tuesday — Moroni 10:8-25 What spiritual gifts have I been given? How can I develop them?

Wednesday — Moroni 10:26-34 Does Moroni's counsel on how to "come unto Christ" help me understand what the phrase truly means?

Thursday — After completing the Book of Mormon what are my overall impressions?

Moroni 10

Friday — What is the most important thing I learned this year?

Saturday — How has reading the Book of Mormon helped me come unto Christ?

Sunday Reflection

Spiritual Promptings

Goal for Next Week

Dec 23-29

Monday

1 Nephi 11:13-36; Mosiah 3:5-10; Helaman 14:1-13 What impressions about Christ and His birth do these verses offer/give me?

Tuesday

Christmas Videos in Gospel Library What videos did I like? What inspired me?

Wednesday

Christmas Music Collection in Gospel Library What phrases in the music helped me feel my Savior's love?

Thursday

2 Nephi 2:6; Alma 7:7-13; 11:40; Helaman 5:9; 14:16-17 How do these passages about Christ's redeeming mission inspired me and make me feel gratitude toward Him?

Christmas

Friday

1 Nephi 6:4; 19:18; 2 Nephi 25:23; 26; 33:4-10 How do these verses testify of Christ?

Saturday

A Living Witness of the Living Christ What truths about Christ could or have changed my life?

Sunday Reflection

Spiritual Promptings

Goal for Next Week

Thank you so much for your purchase! As an author and small publisher, I appreciate it. Make sure to check out my other books of interest at

joyfulsaintspress.com

I have a variety of study guides and journals for adults and children that can help you and your family enhance your Come Follow Me spiritual journey. I also have fun coloring books and word searches that align with the Come Follow Me scripture schedule.

Check out the bonus coloring pages on the next few pages.
Enjoy coloring!

And all thy children shall be taught of the Lord; and great shall be the peace of thy children. 3 Nephi 22:13

WANT MORE FREE COLORING PAGES?

Go to https://bit.ly/36hG5GL to sign up & download

Know ye not that ye are in the hands of God? Know ye not that he hath all power, and at his great command the earth shall be rolled together as a scroll? Mormon 5:23

Made in the USA
Middletown, DE
11 January 2024

47641898R00071